When the HOLY SPIRIT *Speaks*

JOAN ROWLEY-HI

When the Holy Spirit Speaks

Published by Exodus Christian Book Publishing
www.exoduschristianbookpublishing.com

ISBN 9781983516207
Printed in USA

ACKNOWLEDGMENTS

I dedicate this book to

Jesus Christ the Lord and Savior of my life
My Heavenly Father, whom through the Holy Spirit, has given me the inspiration to write When the Holy Spirit Speaks.

Father, in Your precious name, thank You for Your breath of life and the fresh anointing that You have placed on my life. I thank You Father, for Your anointed vessels that You have placed in my life, that have spent countless hours working with me to put together the pages of this anointed book from beginning to end.

A Very Special Thanks to my husband Ronald B. Hill!

Pam, thank you for all the late-night prayers and comfort. Yasmin, thank you for reading, proofing, editing, and your endless words of encouragement. You are my sister in Christ. May God bless you!

A special thanks to my sisters who have served in my life as "GOD's Appointed and Anointed Angels". Barbara and Debbie, you two are the Breath of a Fresh Wind - I thank you both for inspiring me to "Keep My Faith" and "Hold Firm to God's Word". May God bless you both! To my sons Christian, Marvin Jr., and Christopher thank you for reminding mom that "I can do all things through Christ Jesus who strengthens me!" May God bless you!

Father, I pray that this book will touch the thousands of lives who purchase this book. I speak now into existence that someone's life will be changed, charged, healed, delivered and set free through the reading and instructions of "**When The Holy Spirit Speaks**."

TABLE OF CONTENTS

PREFACE

Walking in the Spirit of God is a daily life-fulfilling journey, where you reside in His grace and His mercies. Learning to walk with Him through prayer, fastening, and supplication, allows the Holy Spirit to unveil Himself to you.

As you, commit yourself to walking with GOD, the *Holy Spirit* will give you a different understanding and view of life. As Christians, we are to live a Christlike life, walking in the fulfillment of God. To be filled with the Holy Spirit means that we walk with His *Power! "Ye shall receive power after the Holy Ghost shall come upon you" (Acts 1:8 KJV).* The Holy Spirit sets boundaries for you. You will stop doing things that are not pleasing to God, because the Holy Spirits restricts you from them. The Holy Spirit gives you the peace that surpasses all understanding, and whatever you are wrestling with, you will overcome.

In fact, every opposition you face, God gives you the strength to become *Victorious!* In other words, it is in His might and His power that you will do great things in His name. Did He not tell you that? "I can do all things through Christ Jesus who gives me strength."

God gives you *STRENGTH* for the Journey.

No burden! and No problem! is too big for God.
Remember he is the burden barrier!

Therefore, put on the Whole Armor of God! For truly He has given you a promise, that He will never leave you, nor will He forsake you. As you pray and fast on His word, God will release His revelation to you through the *Holy Spirit.* Allow Him to guide you through your life difficulties as well as your life struggles. Allow Him to prepare you for challenges that you are not capable of facing on our own. God is your anchor! Be still and know that He is GOD!

OVERVIEW

We serve an Awesome GOD! My mother's favorite quotes "What a mighty God we serve" Amen. When we walk in the fullness of Him, we walk in the supernatural realm called *God's Timing.*

PRAYER

Father I pray that this book will touch the thousands of lives who purchase this book. I speak now into existence that someone's life will be changed, charged, healed, delivered and set free through the reading and instructions of *"When the Holy Spirit Speaks"*.

Walking in Gods Perfect Timing!

"To everything,
there is a season,
and a time to every
Purpose under the heaven."
Ecclesiastes 3 (KJV)

Walking in God's Perfect Timing!

There is no better place to be walking, than in "Gods Perfect Timing." Man moves in the *Chronos Timing* and God moves in the *Kairos Timing*. The two are both words from the Ancient Greek vocabularies, yet there is significant difference between the two. To explain briefly, the *Chronos Timing* is described as a timing of chronological order or time in sequence. For example, we can refer it to the timing of a clock, which is measured in seconds, minutes, hours, and years. On the other hand, when you are in daily communion and interaction with the Holy Spirit, it is within this timing called the *Kairos Timing* that our perspectives are pushed beyond the *Natural Realm* of man into the *Supernatural Realm* of God. This is <u>*God Appointed Time*</u> and <u>*Purpose*</u> where He moves in the spirit realm on our behalf. In other words, this is *God's Perfect Timing*! The timing where we begin to walk in faith, trust, and have the confidence of who and whom we are in Christ Jesus. Praying and fastening in this *Timing* allows entrance to walk in Heaven's *Supernatural Realm*.

"My time has not yet come
but your time is always here."
John 7:6 (KJV)

As it is written, in the book of Genesis, Jacobs falls asleep and discovers a hidden mystery of God—a ladder that extends from earth to Heaven. The top of the ladder touches Heaven and there is a movement in the atmosphere, a host of *Angelic Angels* ascending and descending to and from the gates of Heaven. (see Genesis 28:18) Jacob has realized that he has not only uncovered one of the many mysteries of Heaven. but has tapped into the Supernatural Natural Realm of God. Walking in *God's Perfect Timing* allows you to tap into those same mysteries of Heaven. Moreover, when you walk within the harmony and the rhythm of God's Holy Place, you dwell within His presence. As you pray and fast daily, the Holy Spirit will intercede on your behalf. Like Jacob, God will unveil these same mysteries of Heaven to you.

Reflections

Wait on God's Perfect Timing!

"But they that wait upon the LORD
shall renew their strength;
they shall mount up with wings as eagles;
they shall run, and not be weary;
and they shall walk,
and not faint."
Isaiah 40:31 (KJV)

Wait on God's Perfect Timing!

When you wait on God, He renews your strength no matter what the circumstances are, and no matter what we are facing. You can depend on GOD to see you through. God is our ultimate hope in our very time of need. Finding strength in Him gives you peace in all of your life situations. When you "Wait on God", you rest in His power and His might, eliminating all doubts and all of your fears. It does not matter how long you wait – waiting on Him is worthwhile. The wait brings to you rewards and blessings. If He can rescue Daniel in the lion's den, and the three Hebrews boys (Shadrach, Meshach, Abednego) from the fiery furnace, Beloved, He can surely rescue you. Trust in *God's Perfect Timing* in your time of need. Isaiah describes waiting on God, and how He brings rewards toward the very end. Yet, I like to think of it as going to your favorite restaurant and waiting on your server. The overall anticipation in "waiting" keeps you on edge. Yet, once your meal arrives you discover that is was well worth your wait.

"But they that wait upon the LORD shall renew their strength; they shall mount up with wings as eagles; they shall run, and not be weary; and they shall walk, and not faint." Isaiah 40:31 (KJV)

God renews our strengths daily; He removes our weak areas and empowers us with His strength and His might. (Ephesians 6:10 KJV) Finally, my brethren, be strong in the Lord, and in the power of His might. As you fast pray and read your Bible daily, He will truly renew your strength, and as you become renewed you will begin to trust Him in your everyday life decisions. He intensifies your faith to jump over the hurdles and through the obstacles of life, which will cause you to mount up on eagle's wings.

Reflections

My Purpose towards Destiny
The Power to Push

"But ye shall receive power,
after that the Holy Ghost
is come upon you:"
Acts 1:8 (KJV)

My Purpose towards Destiny
The Power to Push

Beloved, no matter what battles you face, God promises in His Word that you are anointed for the battle. Every trial that you have faced, or facing becomes a testimony, and every testimony becomes your revelation of how you made it through. When you walk in *The Holy Spirit,* you are drawn close to the God almighty—depending on His strength and His Word. For our Heavenly Father has expressed that, "Ye shall receive power after the Holy Ghost has come upon you" (Acts 1:8 KJV). The Holy Ghost power is the power that will push you beyond unreasonable circumstances. The circumstances of doubt, fear, sickness, trouble, pain, and any type of personal issues that cause you to miss God's Glory on your life. God will guide you through, if you will just allow Him to be the *Captain of your ship!*

As my mother would say, *"Those unseen hands of God."* **"Come unto me, all ye that labor and are heavy laden, and I will give you rest."**
Matthew 11:28 (KJV)

For our God never sleeps! He will pick you up, and your many burdens will be lightened. Did He not say in His Word That all who labor and are heavy laden—come to Him that He will give you rest? When you enter into God's rest, you will discover that there is no greater peace than having been comforted by His love, His peace, and His Joy. Jesus will calm the raging storms in your life and give you ***The Power to Push!***

Reflections

Fight to Flight!

"But as it is written,
Eye hath not seen nor ear heard,
neither have entered into the heart of man
the things which God hath
prepared for them that love him."
1 Corinthians 2:9 (KJV)

Fight to Flight!

You do not know all the things in which God has in store for you. When you are walking in the presence of God, there is nothing that He shall withhold from you. God will guide you and direct you through the unseen things in life. He will summon you into His glorious presence and reward you just because He loves you.

A battle is not a fight unless you have won the victory. In essence, every battle and every fight brings on a *Victory Praise.* We are certainly *Victorious* in His Name, Amen! Let's provide some Bible wisdom; in the book of Kings, the Bible describes how God provides an army of angels leading horses and chariots of fire to protect Elisha and his servants. In the midst of the flight, He opens the servant's eyes to unveil His host of the angelic army—angels to flight on behalf of His servant.

"For he shall give his angels charge over thee, to keep thee in all thy ways." Psalm 91:11 (KJV)

Now, I have always loved to see the Verizon commercial when you sign up for their phone plan you sign up with a network. Imagine the plan of Jesus.

When you sign up with Him, you sign up with a host of His angelic angels and much more! God gives His angels orders concerning you to protect you in all His ways. The same as He did with Elisha and his servants, God has already done the same for you. His angels will protect you and guard you in all your ways while walking within the obedience to GOD. Finally, when you walk in His obedience, surely GOD will take you from *Fight to Flight!*

Reflections

A New Challenge!

"The LORD is my light and my salvation—
whom shall I fear?
The Lord is my stronghold of my life—
of whom shall I be afraid."
Psalm 27:1 (KJV)

A New Challenge!

The Lord thy God is my everything! He is my counselor in difficult times, my comforter in my distress, and my light in dark places. The very presence of God, His promise given to all humankind, and His readiness to hear our prayers, demonstrates His love that He has for us. God will take a difficult situation and turn it around to simply allow it to work for your good. When you are facing challenges in your life turn to GOD and anchor yourself in His word, allowing His grace and His mercy to carry you through. King David wrote this Psalm when his adversaries tried to overtake him.

"The Lord is my strength and my shield; my heart trust in him, and he helps me. My hearts leaps for joy, and with my song I praise him."
Psalm 28:7 (NIV)

Challenges are just simply an obstacle that hinders and stands in the way of where GOD is taking you. David faced many challenges all around him. Yet his confidence and trust was in God. Moreover, throughout David's process of trials he remembered that in the past God had always brought him through. And rarely do we realize what it means to have strength in GOD. So many times we depend on our own strength and our own wisdom that we begin to lose sight of GOD, who has the *Greater Strength!* One of King David's desires, was to be in His presence daily. When you are in the presence of GOD, He gives you the ability to go through every obstacle that can stand in your way. In fact, your challenges become experiences that help you grow in Christ Jesus.

Reflections

A New Charge!

"Wherefore I put thee in remembrance
that thou stir up the gift of God,
which is in thee by the
putting on of my hands."
2 Timothy 1:6 (KJV)

A New Charge!

A *Charge* is a challenge! It stirs up your walk with God to take your place in what God has called you to do. When GOD places His hand over your life, you are charged to do great works in His name. As you began to do these great works, God will anoint you with the power of the Holy Ghost to perform signs, miracles, and wonders in His name.

 Wow! What an Awesome God We Serve!

Jesus himself performed thirty-seven miracles, signs, and wonders as it has been recorded, throughout the four Gospels of Mark, John, Luke, and Mathew. He healed the sick, casted out evil spirits, and performed many other astounding miracles. As you meditate on the Word of God, the Holy Spirit will uncover the mysteries of Heaven, and reveal to you the charge that He has placed over your own life. When we seek the face of God and we walk in His presence, we walk in love, peace, and joy with an understanding that the spirit of fear does not make us timid but gives us the power to walk in His grace. Paul emphasized to Timothy to stir up the gift of God, which is in you through the laying on the hands. (see 2 Timothy 1:6) This is the gift, which Timothy had received through the Holy Spirit, which was the power to preach and defend the truth of God.

When Apostle Paul spoke, he simply added fuel to the fire when he summoned Timothy to "stir up the gifts." God reassures us in His word that gifts will be stirred up in you as you receive the *Power the Holy Ghost*—He places a charge over your life. Amen.

Reflections

Push to Purpose!

"And we know that all things
work together for good to them
that love God,
to them who are the called
according to his purpose."
Romans 8:28 (KJV)

Push to Purpose!

All things work for the good of those who love Him and for those who are called by Him. When you love God, He will work it all out for your good and call you into your purpose. I'd like to refer to Apostle Paul when he said, "...that in order to move forward in God and to seek after my purpose, I first must forget those things which are left behind and press forward to the goal of the prize." Seeking the face of GOD daily allows you to walk in His spirit. The Holy Spirit then begins to reveal to you the purpose and the plans in walking in your destiny.

"Brethren, I count not myself to have apprehended: but this one thing I do, forgetting those things which are behind, and reaching forth unto those things which are before."
Philippians 3:13 (KJV)

Apostle Paul knew about pressing forward and forgetting those things, which were to be left behind from all that he had been through. He mentions in his writing, to not count himself as having been apprehended. With explanation, Paul's trust in God had changed his course and the outcome of his pursuit to his final destiny in serving God. His desires in life changed to what God wanted. In reality, when God calls you to your purpose, destiny becomes your outcome. In serving God, you take hold of the passion and drive to serve Him and His will becomes your will. Just like Apostle Paul, GOD is calling you to do greater works *pushing you into your purpose.*

Allow Him to bring you from *PUSH to PRESS!*

Push to Purpose!

Reflections

Anointed for the Battle!

"So Samuel took the horn of oil and
anointed him in the presence of his brothers,
and from that day on
the Spirit of the LORD
came powerfully upon David."
1 Samuel 16:13 (NIV)

Anointed for the Battle!

If God be for us, then whom shall be against us! There is nothing in this world that shall stop you from doing the works of God! In retrospect, you are more than a conqueror! In the book of Samuel, God sent the Prophet Samuel on a special mission to anoint David as future King. This special mission that God sent His servant on truly paid off in such an awesome way that David not only became the future King, but was known to God as "A man after God's own heart".

In God's eyes, you are *Anointed for the Battle*! Your battle may bring tears and long nights of walking the floor but God said in His Word that, "Weeping may endure for the night but joy shall come in the morning" (Psalm 30:5 KJV). And what greater joy you will have! Just know that our God delivers and He is a provider, He hears and He knows your every need.

Moreover, even though in this life, we all have to go through certain trials and tribulations God will always be with you and help you get through each and every storm cloud that may come into your life. "Let your conversation be without covetousness; and be content with such things as ye have: for he hath said, I will never leave thee, nor forsake" (Hebrews 13:5 KJV).

"Finally, my brethren, be strong in the Lord, and in the power of his might" Ephesians 6:10 (KJV)

Being strong in God—having the courage to stand in His power and in His might is the ultimate sacrifice. Because it is God Himself who holds the power to fight and win on your behalf. No human power alone can stop the devil's schemes, but God has already disarmed him and put him to open shame by triumphing over him. (see Colossians 2:15) The power of the Holy Spirit, that same power that raised Jesus from the dead, lives in us as believers and gives us the fight to *Win*.

Anointed for the Battle! *Amen*

Reflections

From the Pit to the Palace!

"Then Joseph had a dream!"
Genesis 37: 5 (KJV)

From the Pit to the Palace!

Then Joseph had a dream! From a very young age Joseph believed that God had already, pre-destined him for greatness. We all have dreams no matter what age you are, and dreams are blessings poured out in our lives, made for the future. If you trust GOD and do your part, you will see GOD bring every dream to pass, even if it sometimes seems that your dreams have been shattered. Please know that GOD will always bring your broken pieces together, especially when you remain faithful. Through His grace and His strength, GOD will give you more than enough to keep you going.

Joseph, in the dream that God gave him, saw himself as a leader and his father and his brother bowing down to him. Yet, in reality, Joseph's brothers were very jealous of him. And when he began to tell them of his dream they plotted to get rid of him. His brothers in fact, threw him in the pit only to be sold into slavery. (see Genesis 37:18-28) However, later in Genesis 40-41 we see Joseph in a whole different light. Joseph is moved from the pit to the palace. His entire life begins to change and the dreams in which God had placed in him begin to come to pass.

All too often, we allow Satan to steal our dreams. We allow him to overwhelm us with the issues, problems, and situations brought on by the everyday stressors of life. It seems as if being thrown into a pit is an awful place to be, especially when the people that you love have taken you down that road. Joseph, while in the pit, learned a different strategy—he never gave up on his dreams and put his trust in the hands of the almighty! And that is when GOD gave him favor and moved him ***From The Pit To the Palace!***

Reflections

Armor of God!

"Put on the whole armour of God
that ye may be able to stand
against the wiles of the devil."
Ephesians 6:11 (KJV)

Armor of God!

When we put on the *Whole Armor of God,* we stand against all the tricks and all the schemes in which the enemy tries to plot against us. Satan brings many strategies to try to convince us that we are not worthy of the promises of GOD. *He wants to take you out!* Yet, he also knows what has already be prophesied about him and what is coming soon. (see Revelation 20:10)

"Therefore take up the whole armor of God, that you may be able to withstand in the evil day, and having done all, to stand."
Ephesians 6:13 (KJV)

Battle Preparation - Be alert and ready for *Battle*
"Stand therefore, having girded your waist with the truth, having put on the breastplate of righteousness" (*Ephesians 6:14 KJV*).

Allow the *Truth Gird* you in what is *Right and Truthful*
"And having shod your feet with the preparation of the gospel of peace; above all, taking the shield of faith with which you will be able to quench all the fiery darts of the wicked one" (*Ephesians 6:15 KJV*).

Safeguard your heart - Put up your *Shield of Faith*
"And take the helmet of salvation, and the sword of the Spirit, which is

the word of God; praying always with all prayer and supplication in the Spirit" (Ephesians 6:16 KJV).

Pull your helmet of salvation down tightly to cover your head and lay hold to the *Sword of the Spirit.*
"With all prayer and supplication in the Spirit" (Ephesians 6:17 KJV).

Consistent Prayer with God!

Reflections

Wear Your Coat!

"Now Israel loved Joseph more than all his children,
because he *was* the son of his old age:
and he made him a coat
of *many* colours."
Genesis 37:3 (KJV)

Wear Your Coat!

Joseph's father blessed him with a coat of many colors because he was a wise son to him. Joseph's coat was special. It was interwoven with threads of many patchwork designs that were colorful. The diverse figures and colors must have been beautifully laid out in the artwork form of a patchwork quilt with painted patches throughout the embroidered pieces of various colors. Moreover, when Joseph wore his coat, the sleeves were enough that it covered his hands. And the length of his coat reached his ankles. With all the colors, patterns and patchworks every detail of this special made garment would play a significant role and purpose in Joseph's life as he matured and grew in *God's Grace.*

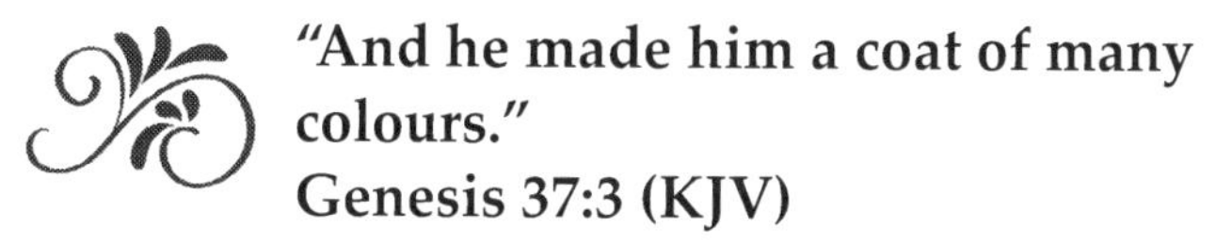

"And he made him a coat of many colours."
Genesis 37:3 (KJV)

Beloved God has designed a special coat for you. Just as Joseph's coat was made special for him – the colors represented the anointing God placed over his life. When Joseph was thrown in the pit by his brothers, he remained humble and God brought him out. He could have become bitter for what his brothers had done to him, but instead he depended on God to bring it to pass. And little did Joseph know that his destiny was being shaped by the hands of GOD. Beloved, the colors of your coat represent your strengths in your trials. Only you can wear the coat that God has designed for you and only you. So wear your designer coat from your Heavenly Father and *WALK INTO YOUR DESTINY!*

Reflections

Through it All God is with You!

"When thou passeth through the waters,
I will be with thee; and through the rivers,
they shall not overflow thee:
when thou walkest through the fire,
thou shalt not be burned;
neither shall the flame kindle upon thee."
Isaiah 43:2 (KJV)

Through it All God is with You!

"Behold, I give unto you power to tread on serpents and scorpions, and over all the power of the enemy: and nothing shall by any means hurt you" (Luke 10:19 KJV). Our God has given you "Kingdom Authority" to advance forward in your assignments in which He has called you to do. Apostle Paul was a prisoner on his way to Rome. And the boat that was carrying him got caught into a storm and was ship wrecked.

Paul and the others aboard held on to the broken pieces and ended up on the Island of Malta. He began to build a fire and as he gathered pieces of wood and put them on the fire, he was bitten by a viper, driven out by the heat. Apostle Paul shook the viper off and continued to go about his Father's business. (see Acts 27: 1-44)

Through it all, he realized that God was with him. As a Christian, you are going to go through the heat of the fire. But just as Apostle Paul shook off the viper and continued to press forward in doing God's works, so shall you. When you come against opposition, "Shake It Off" and trust God!

REJOICE IN THE LORD!

"Notwithstanding in this rejoice not, that the spirits are subject unto you; but rather rejoice, because your names are written in heaven."
Luke 10:20 (KJV)

Reflections

Praying and Fasting

"So we fasted and earnestly prayed
that our God would take care of us,
and he heard our prayer."
Ezra 8:23 (NLT)

Praying and Fasting

There are so many reasons why you should "Pray and Fast." Fasting helps draw you into a more intimate relationship with God. It also helps you to overcome sin, bad habits, and will open your eyes open to the things in your life that are displeasing to God. A time of Praying and Fasting will help separate you from the things of the world, so you come closer to God. It allows you to hear Him better and rely on Him more.

Jesus Expects Us to Fast and Pray!

The Bible has a great deal to say about Praying and Fasting including commands on how to Pray and Fast. The Bible also gives us examples of God leading men and women who prayed and fasted using different types of fasting for different reasons, all of which had positive results. Jesus prayed and fasted. Jesus' disciplines prayed and fasted. The followers of John the Baptist prayed and fasted.

When you Pray and Fast , you learn to humble yourself before the Lord and commit every way unto Him. He shalt exalt you in due time and in due season. Don't fast to brag, or appear spiritual before others – make sure your motives are right and always do it for the glory of God.

"But thou, when thou fastest, anoint thine head, and wash thy face; 18 That thou appear not unto men to fast, but unto thy Father which is in secret: and thy Father, which seeth in secret, shall reward thee openly" Mathew 6:17-18 (KJV).

Fasting and Praying brings Breakthroughs!

Reflections

The Names of God

"And this is life eternal,
that they might know thee
the only true God, and Jesus Christ,
whom thou hast sent."
John 17:3 (KJV)

ELOHIM
Lord God - Mighty One

"God" - The name refers to God's magnificent power and might. He is the One and *Only GOD*. He is the one in whom we can fully rely on. He is the mighty one over all nations. He holds the stars in the sky, and carries His people through difficult times. He is the creator, sustainer, and supreme judge of the world. You can be reassured, the almighty God the holds you, you never have to fear. God's hands are strong and secure.

SCRIPTURE MEDITATION

 "In the beginning, God created the heavens and the earth" (Genesis 1-1 KJV).

 "The heavens declare the glory of God; and the firmament sheweth his handywork" (Psalm 19:1 KJV).

 "Ah Lord GOD! behold, thou hast made the heaven and the earth by thy great power and stretched out arm, and there is nothing too hard for thee" (Jeremiah 32:17 KJV).

YAHWEH

The Lord - Jehovah

"The Lord" – Yahweh is the promise name of God. It is derived from the Hebrew word "I AM" It is the proper name meaning divine person coming from the verb that means "exist, be." God's name Yahweh is one of authority, holds great power, and says all who hear, "I AM the One and true God. You can trust his leadership in your life, just as Moses did in the book of Exodus 3:13-14 when he called him for a specific purpose.

SCRIPTURE MEDITATION

- "And God said unto Moses, I AM THAT I AM: and he said, Thus shalt thou say unto the children of Israel, I AM hath sent me unto you" (Exodus 3:13-14 KJV).
- "God also said to Moses, "Say to the Israelites, 'The LORD, the God of your fathers—the God of Abraham, the God of Isaac and the God of Jacob—has sent me to you.' "This is my name forever, the name you shall call me from generation to generation" (Exodus 3:15 NET).

ABBA
Father

"Father" – Abba is the most intimate form of God's name, showing us His character as our loving father. He is the one who can only be fully trusted, the One you can lean on and the One who cares about all that concerns you. He will give you the strength and covering you will need in your life journey. He will provide the way for you to call out to Him and give you the reassurance beyond doubt and your fears. He *will a*nswer your every call. Especially in your most difficult times that may become too painful in life, you can crawl into the *Heavenly Father's* lap and know that He is for you and His arms will hold you secure.

SCRIPTURE MEDITATION

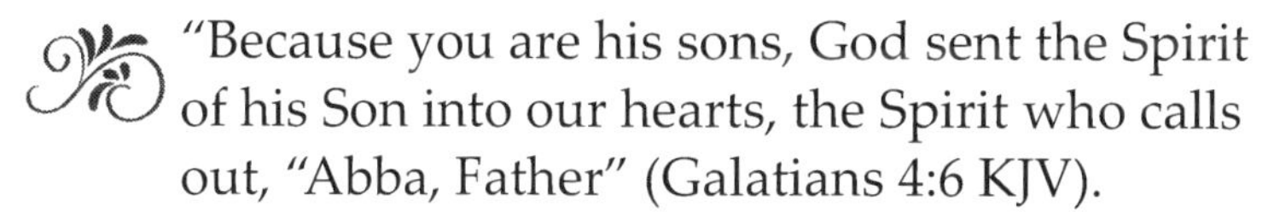

"Because you are his sons, God sent the Spirit of his Son into our hearts, the Spirit who calls out, "Abba, Father" (Galatians 4:6 KJV).

"For ye have not received the spirit of bondage again to fear; but ye have received the Spirit of adoption, whereby we cry, Abba, Father" (Romans 8:15 KJV).

EL ELYON

Most High God

"Most High God" – El Elyon is a name used through the Old Testament revealing God is above all gods. He is indeed the God of Most High, the One who resigns supreme and who is greater than any force of darkness in this world. He is bigger than any problem you might come against. He will never lose His almighty power and might. He is mighty, He is Lord, and He is exalted of all and He shall reign forever.

SCRIPTURE MEDITATION

- "I will praise the Lord according to his righteousness: and will sing praise to the name of the Lord of the Lord most high" (Psalm 7:17 KJV).
- "He blessed Abram, saying, "Blessed be Abram by the Most High God, Creator of heaven and earth" (Genesis 14:1 NET).
- "Glory to God in the highest, and on earth peace, good will toward men" (Luke 2:14 KJV).

EL ROI

The God Who Sees Me

"The God Who Sees Me" – El Roi is a reflection on the love and kindness the points out God's character. The name says that God is watching over everything that He sees including the affairs of His children. He knows when we feel lost and unloved. He is the one who chases after us, who follows you with His goodness. He is the one who sees you when you feel lonely, or when you just need a reminder that God is close. When Hagar had run away to a desert place far from those, she felt hurt and betrayed. God surrounded her in so much grace and care. He did not leave her alone in her troubles. The same as He did with Hagar, He will do the same for you. God will never leave you in your difficult times because He is always close.

SCRIPTURE MEDITATION

"She gave this name to the LORD who spoke to her: "You are the God who sees me," for she said, "I have now seen the one who sees me" (Genesis 16:13 KJV).

EL SHADDAI

Lord God Almighty

"God Almighty" – He is mighty and all-powerful. You can find refuge and rest in His shadow. This is comforting in a world where we face many battles day by day. God's reminder that He is the Almighty that will give you security and assurance that nothing else around you will harm you. He is the God who sees all, knows all, and has the power to go before you, walk with you, and cover you with His grace and mercy. Dwelling in His presence gives you shelter and rest in your time of comfort.

SCRIPTURE MEDITATION

- "He that dwelleth in the secret place of the Most High shall abide under the shadow of the Almighty" (Psalm 91 KJV).
- "Then the Lord said to Moses, "Now you will see what I will do to Pharaoh, for compelled by my strong hand he will release them, and by my strong hand he will drive them out of his land" (Exodus 6:1 NET).

JEHOVAH-JIREH
The Lord Will Provide

"The Lord Will Provide" – God will provide for all your needs. Every one of them, He is faithful, He is able, and there is nothing too difficult for Him. Sometimes His timing is different from ours. Nevertheless, we can trust Him, and His perfect timing. All things are possible for Him even when we you cannot see your way out. Abraham found this to be true. Alone with his son Isaac in the wilderness, he knew and trusted that God would provide for a sacrifice in place of his only child. He believed that God would be faithful. Often it seems that God will test your hearts as He did with Abraham's that day. God will sometimes test you to find out what you are willing to lay down before Him, before he opens the door of provision and blessing.

SCRIPTURE MEDITATION

"And Abraham called the name of that place Jehovahjireh: as it is said to this day, In the mount of the LORD it shall be seen" (Genesis 22:14 KJV).

JEHOVAH-NISSI

The Lord My Banner

"The Lord My Banner" - The name of God proclaims His protection, His leadership, and His deliverance for His people. Just as God brought protection for the Israelites against their enemy the Amalekites, God offers that same protection and deliverance from our enemies that we may be facing today. When Joshua and the people fought against their enemies. Moses stood on the top of a hill with God's staff holding in his hand. The Bible witnesses that even though Moses grew weary in battle when his hands were lifted up the Israelites were winning, and when his hands were lowered the Amalekites were winning. Surely, it is clear by all who gave them the *Victory* on that day. Too many times we spin our wheels trying to balance the hard times in our own strength that we get weary. Yet, Gods reminds that He is our "Banner of Praise" the one that is able to lead us and give us supernatural *Victory*.

SCRIPTURE MEDITATION

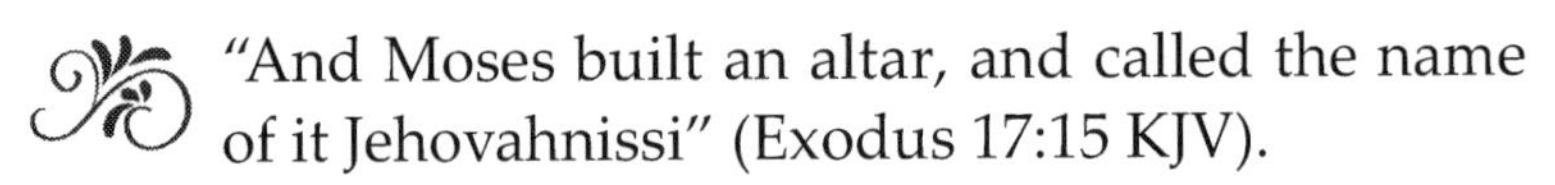

"And Moses built an altar, and called the name of it Jehovahnissi" (Exodus 17:15 KJV).

JEHOVAH-RAPHA
The Lord Who Heals

"Healer, the Lord who heals" – This name brings comfort and hope to many of us who have prayed for healing and deliverance from disease, illness, brokenness, or painful circumstances. It reminds us of how God knows that we need His help. God knows just where you need your healing and deliverance. He promises to redeem every broken place in our lives. He will never leave you to defend yourself. Without Him we could not hope for true freedom and healing. God has brought miraculous deliverance from all types of diseases and difficulties throughout His word. Sometimes the healing does not come in the timetable or way we choose but in God's timing. As believers, we must continue to trust Him and honor His word, and His commands.

SCRIPTURE MEDITATION

"He said, "If you listen carefully to the LORD your God and do what is right in his eyes, if you pay attention to his commands and keep all his decrees, I will not bring on you any of the diseases I brought on the Egyptians, for I am the LORD, who heals you" (Exodus 15:26 NIV).

JEHOVAH-SHALOM

The Lord My Peace

"The Lord My Peace" - God is the only one that is able to give us peace that surpasses all understanding. Gideon knew about "Peace" from the time his people were surrounded by a fierce enemy. God showed up mightily on behalf of Gideon and his people. God brought deliverance out of a time when it should have been fear, but it was "Peace." Perhaps that is why Gideon felt compelled to build an altar to the Lord and call it *"The Lord of Peace."* He knew that in his greatest times of darkness God was there by his side. In a world that seems hard and full of struggles, in the very midst of it all, God reminds us that our true peace is in Him. No matter what you face, remember God is our *Jehovah-Shalom!*

SCRIPTURE MEDITATION

"Then Gideon built an altar there unto the LORD, and called it Jehovah shalom: unto this day, it is yet in Ophrah of the Abiezrites" (Judges 6:24 KJV).

JEHOVAH-RAAH
The Lord My Shepherd

"The Lord My Shepherd; I shall not want. A shepherd is one who feeds or leads his flock to pasture. The name proclaims that God is our personal shepherd that leads and guides us as we place our trust in Him. In Psalm 23, David referred to *Jehovah-Raah* as being his personal shepherd that in his time of need God provided his tender care. We are God's flock and He is our Shepherd who provides for us. When you put your trust in Him, and confess that He is your Lord and Savior, you never have to wonder which way you should go. Because He will lead you through the struggles of life, and protect you from fear and danger.

SCRIPTURE MEDITATION

- "The Lord is my shepherd; I shall not want. He makes me lie down in green pastures. He leads me beside the quiet waters. He restores my soul. He leads me in the path of righteousness for his namesake" (Psalm 23:1-3 KJV).
- "For in a time of trouble He shall hide me in his pavilion; In the secret place of his tabernacle He shall hide me; He shall set me high upon a rock." (Psalm 27:5 NKJV).

BIBLICAL SCRIPTURES

Spiritual Survival Guide

Trusting God

"**Trust In the LORD with all with all your heart**, And lean not on your own understanding; In all thy ways acknowledge Him, and He shall direct thy path" (Proverbs 3-6 KJV).

"**Fear not, for I am with you**; Be not dismayed, for I am your God. I will strengthen you, Yes, I will help you, I will uphold you with My righteous right hand" (Isaiah 41:10 KJV).

"**The Heart of man plans his way** but the LORD establishes his steps" (Proverbs 16:9 ESV).

"**I can do all things through Christ Jesus**, which strengthens me" (Philippians 4:13 KJV).

"**But they that wait upon the LORD** shall renew their strength; they shall mount up with wings as eagles; they shall run, and not be weary; and they shall walk, and not faint" (Isaiah 40:31 KJV).

"**Now faith is the substance of things hoped for**, the evidence of things not seen" (Hebrews 11:1 KJV).

"**He that trusteth in his own heart is a fool**: but whoso walketh wisely, he shall be delivered" (Proverbs 28:26 KJV).

"**For his anger endureth but a moment**; in his favour [is] life: weeping may endure for a night, but joy [cometh] in the morning" (Psalm 30:5 KJV).

"**But now thus saith the LORD that created thee**, O Jacob, and he that formed thee, O Israel, Fear not: for I have redeemed thee, I have called [thee] by thy name; thou [art] mine" (Isaiah 43:1-4 KJV).

"**For I say, through the grace given to me**, to everyone who is among you, not to think *of himself* more highly than he ought to think, but to think soberly, as God has dealt to each one a measure of faith" (Romans 12:3 KJV).

"**Therefore I say to you, whatever things you ask when you pray**, believe that you receive *them,* and you will have *them" (*Mark 11:24 NKJV).

"**My son, do not forget my teaching**, but let your heart keep my commandments, for length of days and years of life and peace they will add to you. Let not steadfast love and faithfulness forsake you; bind them around your neck; write them on the tablet of your heart. So you will find favor and good success in the sight of God and man. Trust in the LORD with all your heart, and do not lean on your own understanding" (Proverbs 3:1-5:6 ESV).

Reflections

God's Direction

"**I will instruct thee and teach thee** in the way which thou shalt go: I will guide thee with mine eye" (Psalm32:8 KJV).

"**The steps of a [good] man are ordered by the LORD**: and he delighteth in his way" (Psalm 37:23 KJV).

"**For I know the thoughts that I think toward you, saith the LORD**, thoughts of peace, and not of evil, to give you an expected end" (Jeremiah 29:11 KJV).

"**And the spirit of the LORD shall rest upon him**, the spirit of wisdom and understanding, the spirit of counsel and might, the spirit of knowledge and of the fear of the LORD" (Isaiah 11:2 KJV).

"**Call unto me, and I will answer thee**, and shew thee great and mighty things, which thou knowest not" (Jeremiah 33:3 KJV).

"**But the LORD said unto me, Say not, I am a child**: for thou shalt go to all that I shall send thee, and whatsoever I command thee thou shalt speak" (Jeremiah 1:7-8 KJV).

"**The preparations of the heart** in man, and the answer of the tongue, [is] from the LORD" (Proverbs 16:1-2 KJV).

"**Thus saith the LORD, which maketh a way** in the sea, and a path in the mighty waters; Which bringeth forth the chariot and horse, the army and the power; they shall lie down together, they shall not rise: they are extinct, they are quenched as tow. Remember ye not the former things, neither consider the things of old. Behold, I will do a new thing; now it shall spring forth; shall ye not know it? I will even make a way in the wilderness, and rivers in the desert" (Isaiah 43:16-19 KJV).

"**Blessed is the man whom thou chastenest**, O LORD, and teachest him out of thy law" (Psalm 94:12 KJV).

"**He restoreth my soul**: he leadeth me in the paths of righteousness for his name's sake" (Psalm 23:3 KJV).

"**Thus saith the LORD**, thy Redeemer, the Holy One of Israel; I am the LORD thy God which teacheth thee to profit, which leadeth thee by the way [that] thou shouldest go" (Isaiah 48:17 KJV).

Reflections

Forgiveness

"**And be ye kind one to another, tenderhearted, forgiving** one another, even as God for Christ's sake hath forgiven you" (Ephesians 4:32 KJV).

"**But if ye forgive not men their trespasses**, neither will your Father forgive your trespasses" (Matthew 6:15 KJV).

"**If we confess our sins, he is faithful and just to forgive us** [our] sins, and to cleanse us from all unrighteousness" (1 John 1:9 KJV).

"**Then came Peter to him, and said, Lord, how oft shall my brother sin against me**, and I forgive him? till seven times? Jesus saith unto him, I say not unto thee, Until seven times: but, Until seventy times seven" (Matthew 18:21-22 KJV).

"**For if ye forgive men their trespasses**, your heavenly Father will also forgive you: But if ye forgive not men their trespasses, neither will your Father forgive your trespasses" (Matthew 6:14-15 KJV).

"**Confess [your] faults one to another**, and pray one for another, that ye may be healed. The effectual fervent prayer of a righteous man availeth much" (James 5:16 KJV).

"**But I say unto you which hear, Love your enemies**, do good to them which hate you" (Luke 6:27 KJV).

"**Judge not, and ye shall not be judged**: condemn not, and ye shall not be condemned: forgive, and ye shall be forgiven" (Luke 6:37 KJV).

"**Forbearing one another**, and forgiving one another, if any man have a quarrel against any: even as Christ forgave you, so also [do] ye" (Colossians 3:13 KJV).

"**He hath not dealt with us after our sins**; nor rewarded us according to our iniquities. For as the heaven is high above the earth, so great is his mercy toward them that fear him" (Psalm 103:10-11 KJV).

"**As far as the east is from the west**, so far hath he removed our transgressions from us. Like as a father pitieth [his] children, [so] the LORD pitieth them that fear him. For he knoweth our frame; he remembereth that we are dust" (Psalm 103:12-14 KJV).

Reflections

Strength

“**And he said unto me, My grace is sufficient for thee**: for my strength is made perfect in weakness. Most gladly therefore will I rather glory in my infirmities, that the power of Christ may rest upon me” (2 Corinthians 12:9 KJV).

“**Be strong and of a good courage**, fear not, nor be afraid of them: for the LORD thy God, he it is that doth go with thee; he will not fail thee, nor forsake thee” (Deuteronomy 31:6 KJV).

“**For the LORD your God is he that goeth with you**, to fight for you against your enemies, to save you” (Deuteronomy 20:4 KJV).

“**There hath no temptation taken you** but such as is common to man: but God is faithful, who will not suffer you to be tempted above that ye are able; but will with the temptation also make a way to escape, that ye may be able to bear it” (1 Corinthians 10:13 KJV).

“**Come unto me, all ye that labour and are heavy laden** and I will give you rest” (Matthew 11:28 KJV).

“**Be of good courage, and he shall strengthen your heart**, all ye that hope in the LORD” (Psalm 31:24 KJV).

“The LORD is my strength and song, and he is become my salvation: he [is] my God, and I will prepare him an habitation; my father’s God, and I will exalt him” (Exodus 15:2 KJV).

"**Watch ye, stand fast in the faith**, quit you like men, be strong" (1 Corinthians 16:13 KJV).

"**But seek ye first the kingdom of God**, and his righteousness; and all these things shall be added unto you" (Matthew 6:33 KJV).

"**He gives power to the faint**, and to him who has no might increases strength" (Isaiah 40:29 ESV).

"**The Lord is my strength and my shield**; in him my heart trusts, and I am helped; my heart exults, and with my song I give thanks to him. The Lord is the strength of his people; he is the saving refuge of his anointed" (Psalm 28:7-8 ESV)

"**And we know that those who love God all things work together for good**, for those who are called according to his purpose" (Romans 8:28 ESV).

Reflections

Healing

"**But he was wounded for our transgressions**, he was bruised for our iniquities: the chastisement of our peace was upon him; and with his stripes we are healed" (Isaiah 53:5 KJV).

"**Fear thou not; for I [am] with thee**: be not dismayed; for I [am] thy God: I will strengthen thee; yea, I will help thee; yea, I will uphold thee with the right hand of my righteousness" (Isaiah 41:10 KJV).

"**Heal me, O LORD, and I shall be healed**; save me, and I shall be saved: for thou art my praise" (Jeremiah 17:14 KJV).

"**Behold, I will bring it health and cure, and I will cure them**, and will reveal unto them the abundance of peace and truth" (Jeremiah 33:6 KJV).

"**Who his own self bare our sins in his own body on the tree**, that we, being dead to sins, should live unto righteousness: by whose stripes ye were healed" (1 Peter 2:24 KJV).

"**And the prayer of faith shall save the sick**, and the Lord shall raise him up; and if he have committed sins, they shall be forgiven him" (James 5:15 KJV).

"**Beloved, I wish above all things that thou mayest prosper and be in health**, even as thy soul prospereth" (3 John 1:2 KJV).

"**Confess your faults one to another**, and pray one for another, that ye may be healed. The effectual fervent prayer of a righteous man availeth much" (James 5:16 KJV).

"**The LORD will strengthen him upon the bed of languishing**: thou wilt make all his bed in his sickness" (Psalm 41:3 KJV).

"**He healeth the broken in heart**, and bindeth up their wounds" (Psalm 147:3 KJV).

"**And when he had called unto [him] his twelve disciples, he gave them power** [against] unclean spirits, to cast them out, and to heal all manner of sickness and all manner of disease" (Matthew 10:1 KJV).

Reflections

God's Grace

"**Let us therefore come boldly unto the throne of grace**, that we may obtain mercy, and find grace to help in time of need" (Hebrews 4:16 KJV).

"**And he said unto me, My grace is sufficient for thee**: for my strength is made perfect in weakness. Most gladly therefore will I rather glory in my infirmities, that the power of Christ may rest upon me" (2 Corinthians 12:9 KJV).

"**For by grace are ye saved through faith**; and that not of yourselves: it is the gift of God" (Ephesians 2:8-9 KJV).

"**For sin shall not have dominion over you**: for ye are not under the law, but under grace" (Romans 6:14 KJV).

"**And if by grace, then is it no more of works**: otherwise grace is no more grace. But if it be of works, then is it no more grace: otherwise work is no more work" (Romans 11:6 KJV).

"**But he giveth more grace**. Wherefore he saith, God resisteth the proud, but giveth grace unto the humble" (James 4:6 KJV).

"**But by the grace of God I am what I am**: and his grace which [was bestowed] upon me was not in vain; but I laboured more abundantly than they all: yet not I, but the grace of God which was with me" (1 Corinthians 15:10 KJV).

"**But God commendeth his love toward us**, in that, while we were yet sinners, Christ died for us" (Romans 5:8 KJV).

"**Let us therefore come boldly unto the throne of grace**, that we may obtain mercy, and find grace to help in time of need" (Hebrews 4:16 KJV).

"**And of his fulness have all we received**, and grace for grace." (John 1:16 KJV).

"**For the grace of God that bringeth salvation** hath appeared to all men, Teaching us that, denying ungodliness and worldly lusts, we should live soberly, righteously, and godly, in this present world; Looking for that blessed hope, and the glorious appearing of the great God and our Saviour Jesus Christ" (Titus 2:11-14 KJV).

"**Thou therefore, my son, be strong in the grace** that is in Christ Jesus" (2 Timothy 2:1 KJV).

"**The Lord is not slack concerning his promise**, as some men count slackness; but is longsuffering to us-ward, not willing that any should perish, but that all should come to repentance" (2 Peter 3:9 KJV).

Reflections

Prayer & Fasting

"**Be careful for nothing; but in every thing by prayer** and supplication with thanksgiving let your requests be made known unto God" (Philippians 4:6 KJV).

"**If ye abide in me, and my words abide in you**, ye shall ask what ye will, and it shall be done unto you" (John 15:7 KJV).

"**Therefore I say unto you, What things soever ye desire**, when ye pray, believe that ye receive [them], and ye shall have [them]" (Mark 11:24 KJV).

"**Pray without ceasing**" (1 Thessalonians 5:17 KJV).

"**Likewise the Spirit also helpeth our infirmities**: for we know not what we should pray for as we ought: but the Spirit itself maketh intercession for us with groanings which cannot be uttered" (Romans 8:26 KJV).

"**But thou, when thou prayest, enter into thy closet**, and when thou hast shut thy door, pray to thy Father which is in secret; and thy Father which seeth in secret shall reward thee openly" (Matthew 6:6 KJV).

"**But when ye pray, use not vain repetitions**, as the heathen do: for they think that they shall be heard for their much speaking" (Matthew 6:7 KJV).

"**And I say unto you, Ask, and it shall be given you**; seek, and ye shall find; knock, and it shall be opened unto you" (Luke 11:9 KJV).

"**Call unto me, and I will answer thee**, and shew thee great and mighty things, which thou knowest not" (Jeremiah 33:3 KJV).

"**Watch and pray, that ye enter not into temptation**: the spirit indeed [is] willing, but the flesh [is] weak" (Matthew 26:41 KJV).

"**For [there is] one God, and one mediator** between God and men, the man Christ Jesus" (1 Timothy 2:5 KJV).

"**Confess [your] faults one to another**, and pray one for another, that ye may be healed. The effectual fervent prayer of a righteous man availeth much" (James 5:16 KJV).

"**Praying always with all prayer and supplication in the Spirit**, and watching thereunto with all perseverance and supplication for all saints" (Ephesians 6:18 KJV).

Reflections

Selah!
My 21 Days with The King

Meditate on His Word
Day and Night

Day 1

Day 2

Day 3

Day 4

Day 5

Day 6

Day 7

Day 8

Day 9

Day 10

Day 11

Day 12

Day 13

Day 14

Day 15

Day 16

Day 17

Day 18

Day 19

Day 20

Day 21

Prayer of Salvation

Dear God in Heaven, I come to You in the name of Jesus. I acknowledge to You that I am a sinner, and I am sorry for my sins and the life that I have lived; I need Your forgiveness.

I believe that Your only begotten Son Jesus Christ shed His precious blood on the cross at Calvary and died for my sins, and I am now willing to turn from my sin.

You said in Your Holy Word, Romans 10:9 that if we confess the Lord our God and believe in our hearts that God raised Jesus from the dead, we shall be saved.

Right now, I confess Jesus as the Lord of my soul. With my heart, I believe that God raised Jesus from the dead. This very moment I accept Jesus Christ as my own personal Savior and according to His Word, right now I am saved.

Thank you Jesus for Your unlimited grace, which has saved me from my sins. I thank You Jesus that Your grace never leads to license, but rather it always leads to repentance. Therefore, Lord Jesus transform my life so that I may bring glory and honor to You alone and not to myself.

Thank You Jesus for dying for me and giving me eternal life.

Amen

Made in the USA
Middletown, DE
21 February 2024